The FBI's Most Wanted

Back Forward Home Reload Images Open Print Find Stop

Location : http://www.fbi.gov/mostwant/tenlist.htm

What's New? What's Cool? Destinations Net Search People Software

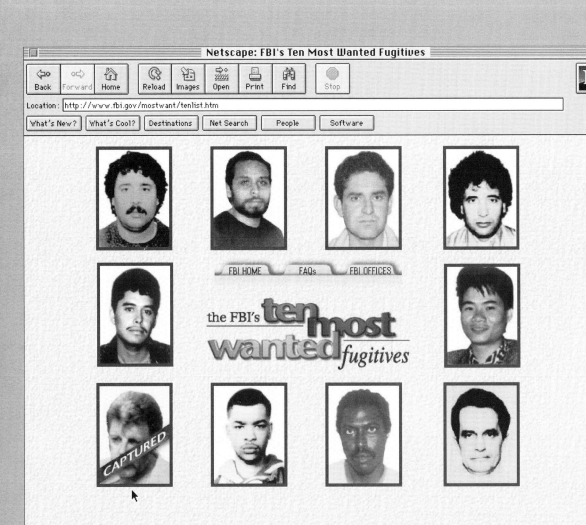

FBI HOME   FAQs   FBI OFFICES

the FBI's **ten most wanted** *fugitives*

CRIME, JUSTICE, AND PUNISHMENT

The FBI's Most Wanted

Laura D'Angelo

Austin Sarat, GENERAL EDITOR

CHELSEA HOUSE PUBLISHERS
Philadelphia

Chelsea House Publishers

Editorial Director Richard Rennert
Production Manager Pamela Loos
Art Director Sara Davis
Picture Editor Judy Hasday
Senior Production Editor Lisa Chippendale

Staff for THE FBI'S MOST WANTED

Senior Editor John Ziff
Editorial Assistant Kristine Brennan
Designer Takeshi Takahashi
Picture Researcher Alan Gottlieb
Cover Illustration Sara Davis

First Printing

1 3 5 7 9 8 6 4 2

Library of Congress Cataloging-in-Publication Data

D'Angelo, Laura.
The FBI's most wanted / Laura D'Angelo ; Austin Sarat,
general editor.

   p. cm. — (Crime, justice, and punishment)
Includes bibliographical references and index.
Summary: Explains why and how the FBI decided to create
the list of Ten Most Wanted Fugitives and how the mass
media and ordinary population have become their allies in
the fight against crime.

ISBN 0-7910-4264-2 (hc)

1. Criminals—United States—Biography—Juvenile litera-
ture. 2. Fugitives from justice—United States—Biogra-
phy—Juvenile literature. [1. Criminals. 2. United States.
Federal Bureau of Investigation.] I. Sarat, Austin. II. Title.
III. Series.
HV6785.D35 1997
364.1'092'273—dc21   97-611
[B]   CIP
                                                                      AC

Contents

CRIME, JUSTICE, AND PUNISHMENT

CAPITAL PUNISHMENT

CLASSIC CONS AND SWINDLES

THE FBI'S MOST WANTED

INFAMOUS TRIALS

JUVENILE CRIME

RACE AND CRIME

SERIAL MURDER

VICTIMS AND VICTIMS' RIGHTS

Fears and Fascinations:

An Introduction to
Crime, Justice, and Punishment

By Austin Sarat

e live with crime and images of crime all around us. Crime evokes in most of us a deep aversion, a feeling of profound vulnerability, but it also evokes an equally deep fascination. Today, in major American cities the fear of crime is a major fact of life, some would say a disproportionate response to the realities of crime. Yet the fear of crime is real, palpable in the quickened steps and furtive glances of people walking down darkened streets. At the same time, we eagerly follow crime stories on television and in movies. We watch with a "who done it" curiosity, eager to see the illicit deed done, the investigation undertaken, the miscreant brought to justice and given his just deserts. On the streets the presence of crime is a reminder of our own vulnerability and the precariousness of our taken-for-granted rights and freedoms. On television and in the movies the crime story gives us a chance to probe our own darker motives, to ask "Is there a criminal within?" as well as to feel the collective satisfaction of seeing justice done.

Fear and fascination, these two poles of our engagement with crime, are, of course, only part of the story. Crime is, after all, a major social and legal problem, not just an issue of our individual psychology. Politicians today use our fear of, and fascination with, crime for political advantage. How we respond to crime, as well as to the political uses of the crime issue, tells us a lot about who we are as a people as well as what we value and what we tolerate. Is our response compassionate or severe? Do we seek to understand or to punish, to enact an angry vengeance or to rehabilitate and welcome the criminal back into our midst? The CRIME, JUSTICE, AND PUNISHMENT series is designed to explore these themes, to ask why we are fearful and fascinated, to probe the meanings and motivations of crimes and criminals and of our responses to them, and, finally, to ask what we can learn about ourselves and the society in which we live by examining our responses to crime.

Crime is always a challenge to the prevailing normative order and a test of the values and commitments of law-abiding people. It is sometimes a Raskolnikov-like act of defiance, an assertion of the unwillingness of some to live according to the rules of conduct laid out by organized society. In this sense, crime marks the limits of the law and reminds us of law's all-too-regular failures. Yet sometimes there is more desperation than defiance in criminal acts; sometimes they signal a deep pathology or need in the criminal. To confront crime is thus also to come face-to-face with the reality of social difference, of class privilege and extreme deprivation, of race and racism, of children neglected, abandoned, or abused whose response is to enact on others what they have experienced themselves. And occasionally crime, or what is labeled a criminal act, represents a call for justice, an appeal to a higher moral order against the inadequacies of existing law.

Figuring out the meaning of crime and the motivations of criminals and whether crime arises from defiance, desperation, or the appeal for justice is never an easy task. The motivations and meanings of crime are as varied as are the persons who engage in criminal conduct. They are as mysterious as any of the mysteries of the human soul. Yet the desire to know the secrets of crime and the criminal is a strong one, for in that knowledge may lie one step on the road to protection, if not an assurance of one's own personal safety. Nonetheless, as strong as that desire may be, there is no available technology that can allow us to know the whys of crime with much confidence, let alone a scientific certainty. We can, however, capture something about crime by studying the defiance, desperation, and quest for justice that may be associated with it. Books in the CRIME, JUSTICE, AND PUNISHMENT series will take up that challenge. They tell stories of crime and criminals, some famous, most not, some glamorous and exciting, most mundane and commonplace.

This series will, in addition, take a sober look at American criminal justice, at the procedures through which we investigate crimes and identify criminals, at the institutions in which innocence or guilt is determined. In these procedures and institutions we confront the thrill of the chase as well as the challenge of protecting the rights of those who defy our laws. It is through the efficiency and dedication of law enforcement that we might capture the criminal; it is in the rare instances of their corruption or brutality that we feel perhaps our deepest betrayal. Police, prosecutors, defense lawyers, judges, and jurors administer criminal justice and in their daily actions give substance to the guarantees of the Bill of Rights. What is an adversarial system of justice? How does it work? Why do we have it? Books in the CRIME, JUSTICE, AND PUNISHMENT series will examine the thrill of the chase as we seek to capture the criminal. They will also reveal the drama and majesty of the criminal trial as well as the day-to-day reality of a criminal justice system in which trials are the exception and negotiated pleas of guilty are the rule.

When the trial is over or the plea has been entered, when we have separated the innocent from the guilty, the moment of punishment has arrived. The injunction to punish the guilty, to respond to pain inflicted by inflicting pain, is as old as civilization itself. "An eye for an eye and a tooth for a tooth" is a biblical reminder that punishment must measure pain for pain. But our response to the criminal must be better than and different from the crime itself. The biblical admonition, along with the constitutional prohibition of "cruel and unusual punishment," signals that we seek to punish justly and to be just not only in the determination of who can and should be punished, but in how we punish as well. But neither reminder tells us what to do with the wrongdoer. Do we rape the rapist, or burn the home of the arsonist? Surely justice and decency say no. But, if not, then how can and should we punish? In a world in which punishment is neither identical to the crime nor an automatic response to it, choices must be made and we must make them. Books in the CRIME, JUSTICE, AND PUNISHMENT series will examine those choices and the practices, and politics, of punishment. How do we punish and why do we punish as we do? What can we learn about the rationality and appropriateness of today's responses to crime by examining our past and its responses? What works? Is there, and can there be, a just measure of pain?

CRIME, JUSTICE, AND PUNISHMENT brings together books on some of the great themes of human social life. The books in this series capture our fear and fascination with crime and examine our responses to it. They remind us of the deadly seriousness of these subjects. They bring together themes in law, literature, and popular culture to challenge us to think again, to think anew, about subjects that go to the heart of who we are and how we can and will live together.

*   *   *   *   *

Of all the agencies in the fight against crime, per-haps none is better known or more important than the Federal Bureau of Investigation, the FBI. In film and on television the exploits of the FBI are regularly por-trayed. *The FBI's Most Wanted* tells the story of the FBI's efforts to fight crime by enlisting the eyes and ears of the citizens to identify the criminal. The book explains why the FBI decided to create the list of Ten Most Wanted Fugitives as well as who gets on that list and why. It shows how the creation and use of the list has blurred the boundaries between professional law enforcement and the population. It also tells a wonder-ful story of how the FBI has come to rely on and use the mass media as an ally in the fight against crime.

This book will be fascinating reading for anyone interested in understanding the investigative tech-niques of the FBI and the way those techniques have helped to create, as well as capture, legendary criminals.

"Give Me Your Toughest Guys"

The long criminal career of Nick Montos came to a humiliating end on July 18, 1995. The notorious bandit who twice made the Federal Bureau of Investigation's Ten Most Wanted list was nabbed in an antique store by an unlikely captor: a bat-wielding grandmother.

That bright summer day Montos was on a hunt for jewels. He strode into a Boston shop, pulled a .22 caliber gun with a silencer from a shopping bag, and pointed it at the elderly proprietor.

"If you keep quiet, I won't kill you," he said. Montos had survived Alcatraz and dodged the death penalty. But he met his match in Sonia Paine. A 73-year-old

---

Under heavy guard, George "Machine Gun" Kelly is escorted from a Memphis jail to face kidnapping charges in Oklahoma. The FBI's widely publicized pursuit of "public enemies" like Kelly, John Dillinger, Pretty Boy Floyd, and Baby Face Nelson set the stage for its list of Ten Most Wanted Fugitives.

Polish Jew who had escaped Nazi persecution in 1939, Paine wasn't about to be pushed around.

Glaring at her assailant, she said, "I'll kill you before you kill me."

Montos should have heeded her warning. Instead, he grabbed Paine and secured her hands to a door with plastic handcuffs. Then he started ransacking the store in search of valuables. He knelt down at the safe and fiddled with the lock.

When he made a nasty crack about the quality of Paine's antiques, she got mad.

Paine wriggled free and pushed a silent alarm that notified police. Then she grabbed an aluminum baseball bat and struck Montos over the head, breaking his glasses. The next blow knocked him to his knees. He sprayed her with Mace.

When police arrived, the battle was raging.

"He put the gun to my back and said if I buzzed the officer in, he would kill me. Well, sweetheart, I just didn't listen. I pressed the buzzer," Paine told reporters. "Then he put the gun to the stomach of the officer. Well, honey, I hit him again with the bat and he lost control of his gun arm."

His head in bandages and his feet in hospital slippers, a wounded and woozy Montos stood before a judge the next day. He was charged with attempted armed robbery and assault and battery.

It had been 10 years since Montos had appeared in a courtroom. In 1985 he jumped the $20,000 bail posted by his wife, after he and three Chicago mobsters were charged with trying to rob a jewelry store in Indiana. Montos fled to Greece, where law enforcement officials assumed he had stayed.

His escape didn't land Nick Montos on the FBI's list of Ten Most Wanted Fugitives for a third time, but police hadn't closed the book on the prolific stickup man either.

"For ten years they are looking for him and they

couldn't find him and guess who caught him," Paine gloated.

While it's unusual for a grandmother to nab one of the FBI's toughest thugs, suspects on the FBI's list usually wind up in handcuffs. The program, aimed at using publicity to bag fugitives, has been credited with the capture of 417 of the 444 suspects listed from March 1950 to January 1996.

It all began on a slow news day in 1949. Sam Fogg, a reporter for the International News Service, was searching for a story. He called FBI headquarters and asked agents for names and descriptions of the 10 "toughest guys" they wanted to capture. The resulting stories created a crush of publicity that helped snare two of the men.

FBI director J. Edgar Hoover and his agents had already been elevated in popular culture to the status of heroes. Their battles with so-called public enemies John Dillinger, Pretty Boy Floyd, Machine Gun Kelly, Alvin "Creepy" Karpis, and Baby Face Nelson had a throttlehold on the American imagination. Movie house newsreels and pulp magazines extolled the exploits of Hoover's agents, who were nicknamed "G-men," for government men.

Now the image-conscious Hoover saw an opportunity to further advance his organization's reputation while aiding in its search for fugitives. On March 14, 1950, Hoover decided to create a permanent list of the FBI's Ten Most Wanted Fugitives and distribute it to newspapers across the country.

General stores and post offices in towns small and large displayed wanted posters. Nine of the first 20 fugitives dubbed "Most Wanted" were caught with the help of citizens.

Fugitives on the Most Wanted list served up publicity both coming and going. Every time a name was added to the list, stories detailing the crimes appeared in newspapers throughout the country. When suspects

Nick George Montos had the distinction of twice making the FBI's Most Wanted list before a grandmother ended his criminal career with a baseball bat.

As FBI director from 1924 until his death in 1972, J. Edgar Hoover molded the bureau into one of the most effective law enforcement agencies in the world. Critics have since documented his abuses of power.

were seized, newspapers followed up with more stories.

Hoover used the FBI's fierce anticrime reputation to fortify his personal power during his reign as director, which extended from 1924 to 1972. But tracking down dangerous fugitives wasn't part of the FBI's original mission. President Theodore Roosevelt created the FBI in

1908 to investigate violations of federal law. But the bureau's mandate was so fuzzy that one critic called it "the odd-job detective agency."

At first, the bureau probed offenses like obscenity in literature and interstate shipping of stolen goods. In 1919 the FBI started investigating suspected draft dodgers, labor-union militants, and German spies. The hunt for high-profile bandits was popularized by Hoover.

The first fugitive to top the Most Wanted list was Thomas J. Holden. Newspapers described him as a "killer and mail train robber." Convicted for bank robbery and escape, Holden was paroled in 1947 after 18 years in prison. Two years later, a drunken Holden argued with his wife at a family birthday party. The fight ended when Holden shot her dead, then killed her brother and her half brother.

A national manhunt was launched by the FBI,

The FBI at a Glance

Director: Louis J. Freeh

Headquarters:
Federal Bureau of Investigation
J. Edgar Hoover Building
935 Pennsylvania Ave., N.W.
Washington, DC 20535-0001
(202) 324-3000

Organization:
Headed by a director and a deputy director. Headquarters is composed of nine divisions and four offices. There are 56 field offices, approximately 400 resident agencies, four specialized field installations, and 23 foreign liaison posts.

Annual Budget: approximately $2.5 billion.

Employees (as of July 31, 1996):
Special agents: 10,529
Support personnel: 15,398

Mission:
"To uphold the law through the investigation of violations of federal criminal law; to protect the United States from foreign intelligence and terrorist activities; to provide leadership and law enforcement assistance to federal, state, local, and international agencies; and to perform these responsibilities in a manner that is responsive to the needs of the public and is faithful to the Constitution of the United States."

Motto: "Fidelity, Bravery, Integrity"

which characterized Holden as a "menace to every man, woman and child in America." Holden went underground, assumed a new identity, and wound up as a plasterer in Oregon. A sharp-eyed citizen who recognized Holden's picture from a local newspaper story tipped off the FBI, and G-men captured the fugitive at his job in June 1951. He subsequently was convicted of murder and died in an Illinois prison two years later.

The glare of publicity made it harder for fugitives to hide. In the first 20 years of the Most Wanted list, nearly 36 percent of those caught were found with information from the public.

But not everyone was enthusiastic about the Most Wanted program. Critics, like former FBI agent William Turner, decried the program as a mere publicity stunt. In his 1970 book, *Hoover's FBI: The Men and the Myth,* Turner argued that the FBI used the program to distort the reality of crime, by creating public enemies from an "array of cheap thugs, barroom knifers, psychopathic rapists, wife-beaters, and alcoholic stick-up men."

He said the program deflected attention from the real menace to society: organized crime. Prohibition was the doorway for the national expansion of the Mafia, which grew in power and influence through its control of gambling and drug smuggling. By the 1950s organized crime was thriving in the United States.

In 1951 millions of Americans watched as gangsters appeared on TV before a Senate committee investigating organized crime. After hearing from 800 witnesses, the Kefauver Committee concluded that there was a "nationwide crime syndicate" called the Mafia.

But FBI director Hoover wasn't interested in going after the mob. For three decades Hoover had assured the country that an organized crime network didn't exist. By 1957, however, the Mafia's presence could no longer be denied. Gang wars exploded on the streets of New York, and grisly accounts were splashed across

Anthony J. D'Anna, a Detroit banker and reputed Mafia boss, testifies before the Kefauver Committee, which investigated organized crime. For years, J. Edgar Hoover disputed the committee's 1951 finding that an organized crime syndicate was operating in the United States. The reason, at least one recent biographer has suggested, was that the Mafia blackmailed Hoover with proof of his homosexual activities.

*Thomas Holden (center),
the first fugitive on the
FBI's Most Wanted list, is
led to court.*

newspaper pages everywhere. That same year, police stumbled upon a convention of 63 top Mafia bosses in Apalachin, New York.

Hoover biographer Anthony Summers argued that the director's reluctance to go after the Mafia was rooted in his deepest secret. In his book *Official and Confidential*, Summers wrote that Hoover was a closet homosexual and transvestite whose forbidden forays were captured on film by Mafia bosses. With that evidence in hand, the Mafia was able to keep Hoover and his G-men off the backs of mobsters. At any rate, during the first 20 years of the Most Wanted program, only one organized crime figure was added to the list; it wasn't until the late 1970s that the lineup began to include fugitives with ties to the mob.

The original lists of the FBI's Ten Most Wanted Fugitives read like a who's who of bank robbers, burglars, and car thieves. As the bureau's priorities changed, so too did its Most Wanted suspects.

Making the Lineup

ick Montos was typical of the early crop of featured fugitives. A career of stickups and auto theft led to the brutal robbery of an elderly couple that landed Montos on the FBI's Ten Most Wanted Fugitives list in 1952. He was captured in 1954 and sentenced to 14 years in Mississippi for an earlier burglary.

Two years later, he and a buddy broke out of a Mississippi prison farm by slicing through a door latch with a hacksaw. They tossed blankets over barbed wire, then scaled the fence. The 1956 getaway earned Montos the distinction of making the Most Wanted list twice in a lifetime.

Another early Top Tenner was Frank Lawrence Sprenz. To the FBI, Sprenz wasn't a run-of-the-mill, gunslinging bank robber. He was the "notorious flying bank robber." Sprenz would stick up banks, hop into a helicopter, and disappear into the blue sky. FBI agents stayed on his trail thanks to Sprenz's sentimental habit

Charles "Black Charlie" Harris (shown here) was the oldest man to make the FBI's Most Wanted list. In 1965 Harris, 69, was added to the list for a double murder.

of sending birthday cards to friends and relatives.

Added to the list in September 1958, Sprenz remained at large until April 1959. That's when a helicopter he was piloting was forced to crash-land on the Yucatán Peninsula in Mexico. The flying bandit was picked up by Mexican authorities while he was walking along a dirt road.

Willie Sutton couldn't fly, but he could hide. Known as "the Babe Ruth of Bank Robbers" and "Slick Willie," Sutton made a sport out of burglary and safecracking. His schemes and disguises, like impersonating a police officer during a robbery, earned him another nickname, "Willie the Actor." He managed to escape prison twice, going over one wall at Sing Sing and under another wall at Holmesburg Prison in Pennsylvania.

Sutton enjoyed an unearned reputation as a quipster. When asked why he robbed banks, he reportedly told a journalist, "Because that's where the money is." Sutton later confessed that he wished he'd thought of that remark, but actually the reporter had made it up.

When the FBI identified him as a Most Wanted fugitive in 1950, Sutton had already been on the run for four years. Bank employees who had been held up by three armed bandits fingered him as the leader. In 1952 Sutton was captured after New York City subway rider Arnold Schuster recognized his face from the wanted fliers.

Schuster's keen memory cost him his life. Mafia boss Albert Anastasia, who declared, "I hate squealers," ordered a hit on him. Sutton, who had always boasted that he made off with more than $20 million during his bank-robbing career, died in 1980 a penniless 79-year-old prisoner.

In the late 1960s and early 1970s, bank robbers and car thieves made room on the FBI's Ten Most Wanted list for a new type of fugitive—political radicals.

This was a time of considerable social unrest in the United States. In many areas of the South, opposition

to the civil rights movement remained strong, and violence frequently erupted. But racial turmoil wasn't confined to the South; massive race riots exploded in such places as the Watts section of Los Angeles, Detroit, and Newark, New Jersey. Many black activists had grown impatient with the civil rights movement's traditional tactic of nonviolence. Militant groups such as the Black Panthers now advocated armed resistance to racist oppression.

FBI director J. Edgar Hoover, who had always viewed the civil rights movement with distrust—and had, in fact, launched a secret campaign to spy on black leaders and infiltrate their organizations—became obsessed with stamping out black radicalism. In 1970 Hoover placed Angela Davis, an African-American philosophy instructor and avowed Communist, on the

Bank robber Frank Lawrence Sprenz arrives for his day in court, June 18, 1959. Like Sprenz, who was captured in Mexico after seven months on the FBI's Most Wanted list, many of the early Top Tenners were bank robbers, burglars, or auto thieves. What set Sprenz apart was his getaway vehicle—a helicopter.

Angela Davis, a philosophy instructor and avowed Communist, was one of a spate of African-American and antiwar militants whom J. Edgar Hoover placed on the FBI's list of Ten Most Wanted Fugitives in the late 1960s and early 1970s. She was eventually acquitted on charges of conspiracy, murder, and kidnapping.

FBI's Most Wanted list. That same year he made H. Rap Brown, onetime chairman of the Student Nonviolent Coordinating Committee, a Top Tenner.

But black activists weren't the only group to receive attention from the FBI. As the 1960s wore on, opposition to America's involvement in the Vietnam War mounted. A chorus of voices publicly denounced American policy, demonstrators clashed with police on city streets and college campuses, and activists broke into government offices and destroyed draft cards (the records determining which young men would be called to serve in the army).

In the antiwar movement Hoover saw a threat to the internal security of the United States, and the FBI director stocked the Most Wanted list with antiwar revolutionaries. After a U.S. Army computer center at the University of Wisconsin was bombed, he insisted on adding six names to the Top Ten.

On May 4, 1970, the clash over the war took a bloody turn on the home front. That day, Ohio National Guardsmen opened fire into a crowd of protestors at Kent State University, killing four people and wounding nine.

One woman became a symbol of that chaotic era. Kathy Power, a senior at Brandeis University who had joined the antiwar movement, wound up an accessory to murder.

Power was wanted by the FBI for her part in the shooting of a police officer in September 1970. She and Brandeis alumna Susan Saxe joined forces with three male parolees to burglarize a Boston National Guard armory and rob the State Street Bank in Boston. They had planned to use the stolen money to buy arms for the Black Panthers.

Power was driving the getaway car when one of the men opened fire on a policeman. The bullet killed respected cop Walter Schroeder, widowed his wife, and left his nine children fatherless.

Police nabbed the three experienced criminals right away. Saxe was put on the FBI's Most Wanted list and picked up on a Philadelphia street in 1975 after being spotted by a policeman. She was released in 1982.

Described as "armed and dangerous," Power eluded authorities for years. She assumed a new identity, Alice Metzinger, and slipped into a conventional life. She was a professional chef, married and the mother of a 14-year-old son named Jaime. She and her family lived in a white-shingled house in Oregon. But behind the normal life of Alice Metzinger was a woman consumed by guilt.

Severe depression forced her to seek psychotherapy. At 44, she decided that guilt would control her life until she turned herself in. She hired a lawyer to negotiate her surrender with law enforcement. In a prepared statement, she told reporters, "I am now learning to live with openness and truth, rather than shame and hiddenness."

Power was sentenced to 8 to 12 years in prison. She has the distinction of being the woman on the list the longest time, from 1970 until 1984.

During the time Power was at large, the FBI's focus had changed again. In the late 1970s and early 1980s, a new brand of criminal populated the list: the serial killer.

The most notorious was Ted Bundy. A former Boy Scout and onetime law student with political aspirations, Bundy had confessed to murdering 30 women. He was suspected of slaying 50 more. His intelligence, boyish good looks, and silver tongue lured young women to him as he crisscrossed the country on an odyssey of rape, mutilation, and murder.

Linda Healy was his first victim. On January 31, 1974, she disappeared from her apartment in Seattle without a trace. Police found bloody sheets and a bloodstained nightgown hanging in her closet.

Over the next five months, reports of missing women struck the Seattle area like electric shocks. A

After the bombing of the World Trade Center in New York, Ramzi Ahmed Yousef, the alleged mastermind, was named a Most Wanted fugitive in April 1993. Two years later Yousef was apprehended in Pakistan. Fugitives with international connections have figured prominently on recent Most Wanted lists.

WANTED BY THE FBI

AIDING & ABETTING; IMPORTATION, MANUFACTURE, DISTRIBUTION AND STORAGE OF EXPLOSIVE MATERIALS

RAMZI AHMED YOUSEF

DESCRIPTION

Date of birth: May 20,1967; Place of birth: Iraq (also claims United Arab Emirates); Height: 6'; Weight: 180 pounds; Build: medium; Hair: brown ; Eyes: brown; Complexion: olive; Sex: male; Race: white; Characteristics: usually clean shaven; Social Security Number Used: 136-94-3472 (invalid SSAN); Aliases: Ramzi Yousef Ahmad, Rasheed Yousef, Ramzi Ahmad Yousef,Kamal Abraham, Muhammud Azan, Ramzi Yousef, Rashid Rashid, Kamal Ibraham, Ramzi Yousef Ahmed, Abraham Kamal, Khurram Khan

CAUTION

YOUSEF ALLEGEDLY PARTICIPATED IN THE TERRORIST BOMBING OF THE WORLD TRADE CENTER, NEW YORK CITY, WHICH RESULTED IN SIX DEATHS, THE WOUNDING OF NUMEROUS INDIVIDUALS, AND THE SIGNIFICANT DE-STRUCTION OF PROPERTY AND COMMERCE. YOUSEF SHOULD BE CONSID-ERED ARMED AND EXTREMELY DANGEROUS.

April 1993

pattern started to emerge: the women were young and attractive, with dark, shoulder-length hair parted in the middle. The ones that got away described Bundy's tactics: he hobbled on crutches or wore a cast on his arm, then asked women for assistance. Those who obliged followed him to their deaths.

Bundy was arrested in January 1977, but he fled custody to commit his final killings. He bludgeoned two sleeping women and savagely attacked two others in Florida State University's Chi Omega sorority house.

In February 1978, four days after he raped and killed 12-year-old Kimberly Leach, Bundy's name was added to the FBI's list of Most Wanted Fugitives. It took five days for police to catch up to him. They spotted his stolen license plates in Pensacola, Florida.

In 1989, after nearly 10 years on death row, Bundy was executed in Florida's electric chair.

His homicidal path was followed by other serial killers such as Christopher Wilder, the Florida playboy who launched a murder spree that left eight women dead or missing.

In the 1990s the FBI changed its focus again, spotlighting fugitives with international connections, such as drug kingpins and terrorists.

Ramzi Ahmed Yousef, 27, who at different times claimed to be a Kuwaiti and a Pakistani citizen, was identified as a Most Wanted fugitive in April 1993 for allegedly masterminding the bombing of the World Trade Center in New York City. The bomb, concealed in a rented van in a lower parking lot of the skyscraper, killed six and wounded hundreds. Although the FBI already had a full list of fugitives when the bomb went off, the bureau decided to make Yousef a "special addition," pushing the list to 11.

"He was a terrorist and it was believed that an immediate international effort would aid in his capture," FBI spokesman Nestor Michnyak explained.

After two years on the run, Yousef was seized by Pakistani authorities at a hotel in Islamabad. He had been tailed by security agents since his arrival in that country.

After being extradited to the United States, Yousef was charged with supervising the purchase and assembly of the bomb and planning the operation. Four other men had already received sentences of life imprisonment without parole for their roles in the bombing.

Charles Lee Herron (pictured here) holds the record for the longest time on the FBI's Most Wanted list: 18 years, 4 months.

President Bill Clinton hailed Yousef's capture. "This arrest is a major step forward in the fight against terrorism," he declared. "Terrorism will not pay; terrorists will pay."

The FBI's Most Wanted have included some of the country's most notorious criminals. But sheer ruthlessness doesn't ensure a spot on the list.

The FBI looks for people with lengthy records of committing serious crimes who are considered a "dangerous menace to society." Fugitives must be wanted on federal arrest warrants, which means that they committed a federal crime or crossed state lines to avoid prosecution. Otherwise the FBI has no jurisdiction.

Criminals make the list only if FBI agents believe publicity will help them make an arrest. Fugitives who are already famous usually aren't candidates for the Most Wanted lineup. For example, if O. J. Simpson had remained at large following the killings of his ex-wife and her friend, he probably wouldn't have landed on the list—as a former football star, TV personality, and actor, Simpson could not have avoided being recognized by the public. Similarly, Patty Hearst, the kidnapped newspaper heiress turned bank robber, didn't make the list in 1974. When surveillance cameras captured Hearst holding a submachine gun during a bank robbery committed by the group that had kidnapped

Federal Crimes That Fall Under the FBI's Jurisdiction

The FBI is charged with enforcing all federal laws, except when jurisdiction has been expressly assigned to another government agency. Among the crimes the FBI investigates are:

- Assassination of a president
- Assault or killing of a federal officer
- Espionage, sabotage, and other subversive activities
- Fraud against the government
- Civil rights violations
- Extortion
- Kidnapping
- Bank robbery
- Interstate transportation of stolen goods

her, the Symbionese Liberation Army, the image appeared on newspaper front pages, magazine covers, and TV. This rendered additional publicity unnecessary.

Another criterion is that the fugitive's real identity must be known. The Unabomber, who first struck in May 1978, never made the list because FBI agents didn't know who was behind the series of mail bombings directed at university professors and business leaders that killed 3 people and injured 23 others. Theodore Kaczynski was arrested in April 1996 after his brother, David, informed authorities of his suspicions.

Every time a fugitive is caught, another is added to the list to take his or her place. The FBI director chooses the replacement after mulling recommendations from agents in the field. The FBI is looking for some 6,000 fugitives.

"That number can be overwhelming," FBI spokesman Rex Tomb observed. "The beauty of the Top Ten is it focuses national attention on just 10 individuals."

Most Wanted fugitives have to be interesting enough to generate publicity. Often agents recommend suspects for the list only after information that might lead to a capture has dried up.

Top Tenners are removed from the list only when they no longer fit the criteria. Four people have been taken off the list without being apprehended, including Kathy Power, who turned herself in a year later.

"After so many years have passed, we decide how much of a threat the person is and consider that there are other criminals that we'd like to profile," explained FBI spokesman Nestor Michnyak.

The fugitive on the list the longest was Charles Lee Herron, who eluded capture for 18 years and four months. He was arrested in Jacksonville, Florida, in 1986 for the 1968 slayings of two police officers.

The killings came during a time of racial tensions in Nashville several months before the assassination of civil rights leader Dr. Martin Luther King, Jr. Herron was in a car with four other men when the shots were fired. All four of his companions were caught and convicted, but Herron managed to elude the law.

In 1974 three of the four men escaped from the Tennessee State Penitentiary by dressing in street clothes and sauntering out with a group of visitors. One escapee, Ralph Canady, hanged himself later in a Baltimore prison after being arrested on a drug-related charge.

Another, William Allen, tried to get a driver's license using false information. State troopers went to his listed address and, unbeknownst to them, stumbled upon Herron. Questioned by the troopers, Herron gave them a false name but raised their suspicions. They searched mug shots and found Herron's picture on the Most Wanted list.

Billy Austin Bryant set the record for the shortest stint on the list. He was captured on January 8, 1969, two hours after killing two FBI agents in Maryland. After fingering Bryant in connection with a bank robbery, the agents knocked on his wife's door. Bryant opened fire and escaped. He was found cooped up in the crawl space above a neighbor's apartment.

The oldest person to be placed on the Top Ten list was 69-year-old Charles "Black Charlie" Harris, who was added in May 1965. A reputed moonshiner, Harris

The FBI's Most Wanted: Vital Stats

Average age:	37	Most frequent crime location:	California
Average height:	5'10"	Average distance between crime	
Average weight:	168.5 pounds	scene and place of capture:	
Average time on list:	316 days		approximately 1,000 miles
Longest time on list:	18 years, 4 months	Month during which the most	
Shortest time on list:	2 hours	captures occur:	March
Number of fugitives on list twice:	6	Chance of being captured	
Proportion of women on list		(through 1995):	93.9%
through 1995:	1.57%		

had beaten a murder charge in 1961. After a taste of freedom, he flew into a jealous rage over an ex-girl-friend. He hunted her and her fiancé down in a house tucked away in the woods, shot and killed them both, then torched the house. FBI agents tracked him down six weeks later. When the agents surrounded him in his hiding place, he grinned and told them, "I'm your man."

Only seven women have made the list of Most Wanted. Ruth Eisemann-Schier was the first. In 1968 she and her partner, Gary Krist (another Top Tenner), were sought for kidnapping and extortion. They had abducted the ailing daughter of a millionaire and buried her alive in a box equipped with an air pump. Eisemann-Schier was captured on March 5, 1969, after she applied for a nursing job under an assumed name. A routine check of her fingerprints revealed that she was wanted by the FBI.

Five other fugitives joined Nick Montos in the two-timer category. James Earl Ray was one of them. He was added to the list in 1968 when he was sought for the assassination of Martin Luther King, Jr., and in 1977 when he escaped from federal prison.

WANTED BY THE FBI

KIDNAPING
CHRISTOPHER BERNARD WILDER

FBI No. 541 725 L2

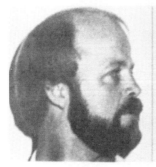   

Photographs taken 1983   Retouched photographs taken 1983

Aliases: Lynn Thomas Bishop, L. K. Kimbriell, Jr., Bernard Christopher Wilder, Chris B. Wilder, Christopher Wilder , Lynn Ivory

DESCRIPTION

Date of Birth: March 13, 1945 (Birth data not supported by birth records)
Place of Birth: Sydney, Australia
Height: 5'11" to 6'
Weight: 175 to 180 pounds
Build: Medium
Hair: Brown (balding)
Scars and Marks: Five inch scar on right ankle
Occupations: Carpenter, contractor, part-time photographer and Grand Prix-type race car driver
Remarks: Usually wears trimmed beard and mustache, may be clean shaven, well spoken and presents a neat appearance , habitual fingernail biter.
Social Security Number Used: 263-19-6634
Florida Drivers' License Number: W43610245093
U.S. Passport Number: 040289030
NCIC: 19TT11COPO151212PI18
Fingerprint Classification: 19 L 9 T 00
                                M 6 U 00 I 18

Eyes: Blue
Complexion: Medium
Race: White
Nationality: American

CRIMINAL RECORD

WILDER HAS BEEN CONVICTED OF SEXUAL BATTERY.

CAUTION

WILDER IS BEING SOUGHT ON FEDERAL CHARGES RESULTING FROM THE KIDNAPING, RAPE AND TORTURE OF A YOUNG FEMALE VICTIM. CONSIDER WILDER ARMED, EXTREMELY DANGEROUS WITH SUICIDAL TENDENCIES.

A Federal warrant was issued on March 22, 1984, at the Middle District of Georgia, Macon, Georgia, charging Wilder with kidnaping (Title 18, U.S. Code, Section 1201).

IF YOU HAVE INFORMATION CONCERNING THIS PERSON, PLEASE CONTACT YOUR LOCAL FBI OFFICE. TELEPHONE NUMBERS AND ADDRESSES OF ALL FBI OFFICES LISTED ON BACK.

William H Webster

DIRECTOR
FEDERAL BUREAU OF INVESTIGATION
UNITED STATES DEPARTMENT OF JUSTICE
WASHINGTON, D. C. 20535
TELEPHONE: 202 324-3000

Entered NCIC
Wanted Flyer 518
April 3, 1984

Manhunt for a Murderer

They were beautiful, young women who often heard that they should be fashion models. Strolling through shopping malls or down beauty-contest aisles, they harbored dreams of being discovered.

He was a millionaire playboy who knew their fantasies. He stepped into their lives promising to splash their pictures on the covers of national magazines and romance novels.

With a camera strapped around his neck and some smooth talk, Christopher Wilder stalked his prey. In the last six weeks of his life, he embarked on a 7,000-mile, transcontinental murder spree that triggered the most intensive FBI manhunt in decades.

The case of Christopher Wilder vividly illustrates the crime-stopping power of the FBI's Most Wanted program. For in the end, what snared the serial killer was not a brilliantly drawn psychological profile or sophisticated police work, but rather national publicity

The FBI's wanted notice for Christopher Wilder depicted the serial killer as photographed with a full beard in 1983 and as he might look clean-shaven or with a mustache.

that the bureau created.

Though Wilder raged with sadistic blood lust, his exterior never betrayed him. The Australian native came across as polite and soft-spoken to neighbors in the Florida coastal town of Boynton Beach. Wilder loved animals. He owned three English setters and made charitable donations to Save the Whales and the Seal Rescue Fund.

He had immigrated to the United States at age 24; by the time he was 39, Wilder had amassed a fortune as an electrical contractor. He lived a life of affluence, running around with fast-lane friends and racing automobiles for sport. Among the cars parked outside his house was a customized Porsche. A speedboat was tethered to his dock. He swam in his screened-in swimming pool and relaxed in a Jacuzzi next to his bed. Inside his home, a photo studio was equipped with special lighting and cosmetics for his models.

Wilder invited women he met at beauty pageants and shopping malls to his home for private photo sessions. In October 1982 he was captured on film by an amateur photographer. He's seen lurking behind contestants at the Miss Florida-USA contest.

That day, Wilder watched women sashay down the runway. He offered to photograph several for a national magazine, then jotted down the phone numbers of those who accepted. It was there that he befriended Elizabeth Kenyon, a 23-year-old finalist in the beauty contest. Kenyon was a student at the University of Miami who worked part-time as a student teacher at a school for the mentally disturbed.

Wilder dated Kenyon for a year and a half. He ingratiated himself with her parents, who found him to be clean-cut and courteous. Wilder grew serious about Kenyon and intended to marry her.

Kenyon didn't know that Wilder had been married in Australia. A few days after the wedding, his distraught bride had packed her bags and left, saying he

had sexually abused her. Nor did she know that as a teenager, Wilder underwent electroshock therapy after he and a group of friends were charged with gang-raping an Australian girl on a beach.

Still, Beth Kenyon rejected his marriage proposals for her own reasons. The main obstacle she cited was the age difference between them; Wilder was 16 years her senior. It has been theorized that something in Wilder snapped when Kenyon turned him down.

The day of the Miss Florida-USA beauty contest, Wilder had also met a 20-year-old model named Rosario Gonzalez. She later told her fiancé that Wilder shot her picture for the cover of a romance book. After that, she never saw or heard from him again—until February 26, 1984, at the Miami Grand Prix.

Wilder competed in the race and came in 17th place. Gonzalez was watching while she worked passing out free samples of a new headache reliever. Witnesses saw her talking with Wilder before she vanished. Her body was never found.

This photo, taken by an amateur photographer at the Miss Florida-USA beauty pageant in October 1982, captured Wilder (at left, with camera) lurking in the background. Two of the contestants he met at the pageant later became his victims.

Less than a week later, Beth Kenyon was seen with Wilder pulling into a gas station in Miami. When she didn't return home from her teaching job, her worried father called Wilder.

"I would never do anything to hurt any of you," Wilder told him on the telephone. Unconvinced by this assurance, Kenyon's father hired a private detective to find out more about his daughter's boyfriend. Meanwhile, Florida authorities were piecing together information on the two missing women. Like Rosario Gonzalez, Beth Kenyon would never be seen again.

On March 13 the *Miami Herald* reported that a Boynton Beach race-car driver was wanted for questioning in the disappearance of two local women. Wilder panicked, dropped off his dogs at a kennel, and set out on a cross-country murder spree.

He snatched Teresa Ferguson from a mall in Merritt Island, Florida, on March 18. The 21-year-old step-daughter of a local police captain, Ferguson was an attractive woman with long, dark hair. She toiled in a factory but dreamed of working on fashion runways and glamorous photo shoots. On March 20 her strangled body was found in a swamp.

That same day, Wilder approached a blond 19-year-old Florida State student in a mall near the school's campus. He offered her $25 an hour to pose for photographs. When she turned him down, Wilder punched her in the stomach and forced her into his car. He beat her and bound her with a clothesline. Then he gagged her, stuffed her into a sleeping bag, and locked her in the trunk of his car.

He drove his hostage to a motel in Bainbridge, Georgia, where he raped her and tortured her with electric shocks, delivered with a 110-volt cattle prod. He tried to seal her eyes shut with glue, but the woman managed to escape to the bathroom and lock him out. Her urgent cries attracted the attention of guests who rescued her. Wilder fled.

The woman later convinced authorities that a serial killer was on the loose. The FBI, which has jurisdiction when a criminal crosses state lines, entered the case. A federal warrant was issued for Wilder's arrest.

The arrest didn't come in time to save the life of Terry Diane Walden, a 24-year-old mother who lived in Beaumont, Texas. Walden dropped off her 4-year-old daughter, Mindy, at a day-care center on the morning of March 23. A nursing student, Walden had planned to study and then go shopping at the local mall. At 5 P.M., when no one came to pick up Mindy, workers at the day-care center called Walden's husband. He later told police that a man had approached his wife about a modeling job a few days before she disappeared. Walden's body was found floating in a drainage canal on March 26.

That same day, fishermen near a lake in Junction City, Kansas, found the body of Suzanne Logan, who had been stabbed to death. The 20-year-old, who had once put together a portfolio of photographs in the hopes of becoming a model, had been abducted from a shopping mall in Oklahoma City.

On March 29 Sheryl Lynn Bonaventura slipped into a pair of cowboy boots, faded jeans, and a white sweatshirt and headed to a shopping mall in Grand Junction, Colorado. Wilder stopped her to say he was looking for a cowgirl type for a modeling assignment. She was never seen again.

Wilder was again caught in the eye of a camera on April 1. The picture, also shot by an amateur photographer, shows him in the background of another beauty contest, at the Meadows Mall in Las Vegas. Following the competition, which was sponsored by *Seventeen* magazine, Wilder left with one of the finalists, Michelle Korfman, a 17-year-old aspiring model. Her body turned up in the Angeles National Forest more than a month later.

Police were compiling reports from other women

Wilder asked Elizabeth Ann Kenyon, a university student and part-time student teacher of the mentally disturbed, to marry him. She disappeared after turning him down.

who had been approached at the Las Vegas mall by a man fitting Wilder's description. Wilder started emerging as the suspect in eight rapes, tortures, and murders of young women in Florida, Texas, Colorado, and Nevada.

On April 3 the FBI added Wilder to its list of Ten Most Wanted Fugitives.

The FBI issues national releases when a fugitive is added to the Most Wanted list, but it rarely summons the national press to a conference. Oliver B. "Buck" Revell, the FBI's assistant director for investigations, took that unusual step on April 5.

"It was a gamble," recalled Revell, now retired. Making too much information public might ruin the government's chance of winning a conviction if Wilder was ever put on trial. But young women had to be warned, and the FBI hoped to stop Wilder in his tracks.

"We don't do national press conferences too often or they lose their impact," Revell said. "But because of the egregious nature of Wilder's crimes we decided to do it. He was very mobile, prowling shopping centers and other areas looking for a particular type of victim.

"We wanted to get information out as quickly as possible and to alert potential victims. We were tightening the circle around him."

At the press conference, Revell told reporters that Wilder "represents a significant danger. He's extremely active, very dangerous, and this approach may lead to his apprehension. He's making contacts on an almost daily basis, and this is potentially a very prolific situation."

Revell released a profile of Wilder and of his victims. He described how Wilder stalked young women.

"After identifying himself as a professional photographer, he comments on a young woman's appearance and attempts to persuade her to accompany him from the area for photography sessions," Revell said. "If rejected, he has beaten and forced victims to accompany him."

Meanwhile, posters with photos of Wilder had been distributed to U.S. border officials and at airports. Police recovered Wilder's Chrysler near Beaumont, Texas. They were closing in.

"We had FBI agents combing motels, diners, and service stations. We tried to learn from each place in the country where he hit. Agents were working behind him and in front of him," Revell recalled.

Only a day before the FBI's unusual press conference, Wilder had abducted Tina Marie Risico, a 16-year-old from Torrance, California, from a mall. For the next three days he kept her bound and gagged. He repeatedly raped her and tortured her with the cattle prod he had used on other victims. But instead of killing her, he made her his accomplice as he looped eastward across the country.

In a hotel room, Wilder forced Risico to watch the TV coverage of the manhunt. He wanted her to know

Special Agent Joseph Corless refers to a map illustrating Wilder's movements during a national press conference announcing the serial killer's addition to the FBI's Most Wanted list. Such press conferences are rare, because making too much information public can jeopardize a case. But the bureau believed that in this instance warning potential victims took top priority.

how dangerous he was. Then he put her to work. He made her approach Dawnette Sue Wilt, 16, in a shopping mall in Merrillville, Indiana. Risico asked her if she wanted to be a model, then led her to Wilder's car to sign consent forms. Wilder pulled a gun and bound and gagged Wilt. She rode in the backseat while Wilder drove toward upstate New York. Held hostage for two nights, she was stabbed and dumped into the woods off a deserted road. Wilder left her for dead.

A farmer driving a truck saw Wilt stumble into the road, bleeding through the clothes she had tied around her chest to stop the flow of blood. He rushed her to the hospital emergency room, where she gave police enough information to put them on Wilder's path.

With the manhunt on the move in New York, Wilder found his final victim: Beth Dodge, a 33-year-old mother who had stopped off at the mall in Victor, New York, on her lunch hour. When Dodge accompanied Tina Risico to Wilder's car, Wilder snatched her and held her captive in the car she had driven to the mall. The body of the young mother was found days later in a gravel pit.

Wilder's final act toward Risico was one of unexplained mercy. He dropped her off at Logan Airport in Boston with more than enough money to buy a plane ticket home. She didn't go straight to police when she returned to California, however. First she went on a shopping spree, spending the rest of the money Wilder had given her.

Meanwhile, Wilder headed north toward Canada. In the small town of Colebrook, New Hampshire, he stopped for gas at Vic Stanton's Getty station.

State Police detective Leo Jellison, who had been following the press accounts of Wilder, noticed something strange about the gold Firebird that pulled in for gas. "I had watched the coverage of Christopher Wilder on TV. It was a major case in the nation and I was somewhat up to speed on it," Jellison recalled.

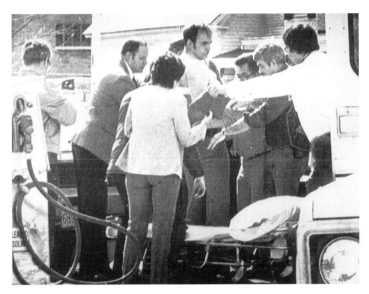

Medical workers help State Trooper Leo Jellison, who sustained a chest wound in his struggle with Christopher Wilder at a Colebrook, New Hampshire, gas station. Wilder died instantly from a bullet fired from his own gun; Jellison recovered.

He remembered the description he had heard of Beth Dodge's car driven by the serial killer Wilder. His suspicion went into overdrive when he noticed that the car's front plate was missing and that the eagle hood ornament was gone.

"I decided to investigate further," Jellison said. The trooper pulled up behind Wilder's car and called out to him.

Wilder ran back to the driver's seat and pulled a gun from the glove compartment. Jellison leaped onto his back and locked him in a bear hug. Wilder's gun went off, sending a bullet through his own heart, and then through Jellison's ribs. A second shot rang out. Wilder was dead.

Surgeons removed a bullet from Jellison's upper chest. After four days in intensive care, he recovered.

Following Wilder's death, some speculated that the serial killer meant to take his own life. But Jellison, who's now a State Police lieutenant in Twin Mountain, New Hampshire, has no doubt about what Wilder intended. "He was going to turn the gun on me," Jellison said.

TRACKING
FUGITIVES ON TV

ob Lord fed the hungry and cared for the homeless with a compassion that concealed his trail of rape and murder.

Lord worked in the same shelter that had helped him get back on his feet when he was a desperate man. In November 1986, Lord had wandered into Project Hospitality, a shelter for homeless people located in a church basement on Staten Island. He told caretakers he had been laid off from a steel company in Chicago and had nowhere else to go.

His enthusiasm and energy quickly set him apart from the others, and it was only a matter of days before Lord was placed in an apartment in a quiet neighborhood.

Devoted to Project Hospitality, Lord turned into a tireless volunteer. He worked around-the-clock doling out food, mopping floors, and making repairs. On cold nights, he steered a van through the streets of Staten Island, searching for people who had no roof of their own. Newcomers to the shelter found a sympathetic ear in Lord and were inspired by his personal story of success.

Tales of his generosity abounded. He dug into his own pockets to give money to homeless people. He built a stage for the shelter's Christmas play and starred as one of the three Wise Men. On Christmas Eve, when two women drifted into the shelter, Lord rushed out to buy them gifts.

When an $18,000-a-year job opened up at the shelter in April 1987, Lord was the logical choice. He was hired to counsel the homeless and help find them permanent jobs and houses. In that role, too, he delivered a star performance.

In the smallest borough of New York City where he lived and worked, Lord had stature. A gifted speaker, he tried to broaden understanding of the homeless by addressing church congregations and schoolchildren.

His picture even appeared in the local newspaper next to an article asking for canned donations to the shelter.

The next time his photo was put before the public eye, it sent a community into shock. On February 6, 1988, Lord's face was featured on a promotion for a new television program, *America's Most Wanted*.

The premiere episode promised to profile prison escapee David James Roberts, who had been convicted of raping a woman and murdering four people in Indiana, including a 2-year-old girl and a 6-month-old boy.

Using dramatic reenactments, *America's Most Wanted* showed how Roberts, out on parole, stole a set of tires from Sears and, fearing that the store manager might recognize him, followed the man home that night. He gagged and strangled the store manager and his wife, then poured a trail of gasoline and set fire to their home. The couple's two-year-old daughter died of smoke inhalation. A three-year-old daughter, who had spent the night at the home of friends, survived.

Roberts was arrested and released on $10,000 bond. The night of his release, he kidnapped a single mother who was driving home from work around 2:30 A.M. The woman had just picked up her 6-month-old son from a babysitter's home. After wrapping him in a blue blanket and packing him into the car, she made her way down the deserted street. Her car stopped at a flashing red light. Startled by a noise, the woman turned and saw a man banging a gun against her car window.

Roberts forced his way into the car, raped the woman, and locked her in the trunk. Then, despite the woman's pleas to spare her baby, Roberts deposited him on the side of the road, where the infant froze to death. Children on their way to school found the baby's body on a snowy lot the next morning. The baby had died clutching blades of grass.

Actors portray David James Roberts and his two guards at the hospital where Roberts was taken for medical tests before his escape. The night America's Most Wanted aired this episode, hundreds of callers provided tips, and the FBI captured the fugitive just four days later, on February 11, 1988.

The real David James Roberts, as seen on the one-year anniversary episode of America's Most Wanted. *From prison, Roberts proclaimed his innocence and asked the show's host, victims' rights advocate John Walsh, how he slept at night knowing he might have helped put innocent people behind bars.*

Roberts was serving six consecutive life sentences when he escaped from the Indiana State Prison in Michigan City in October 1986. Often described as cunning and resourceful, Roberts displayed both those traits in his bold escape.

Roberts had been transferred to a hospital to undergo a pulmonary examination. On the way back to prison, he asked two armed guards to loosen his chains so he could eat fast food in the back of the car. When one of the guards tried to refasten his chains, Roberts whipped out a gun and forced both guards to surrender their uniforms. Roberts would later use the uniforms as a disguise. Grabbing the steering wheel of the car, he drove off with his two captives. The two guards escaped when he stopped to make a phone call.

Weeks later Roberts arrived on Staten Island, where he reinvented himself as the kindly Bob Lord. The month Bob Lord was hired to coordinate shelter programs for Project Hospitality, David James Roberts was added to the FBI's list of Ten Most Wanted Fugitives.

On February 6, when the promotion for *America's Most Wanted* appeared in *TV Guide*, Roberts was laid up in the hospital. Doctors were running tests to determine why he was coughing up blood. They didn't know he had contracted pulmonary histoplasmosis—a disease of the lungs—from eating in the prison dining hall, where pigeon droppings fell into the food.

Roberts didn't stick around for the diagnosis; he checked out of the hospital against medical advice and slipped into hiding.

That night, television viewers on Staten Island were stunned to see the man they knew as dedicated shelter worker Bob Lord described as "armed and dangerous."

The host of *America's Most Wanted* called Roberts a "convincing smooth talker who appears very well educated." Four photographs flashed on the screen. One showed Roberts with wire-rim glasses, another showed him in a suit, and two others showed him in prison blues.

"Take a close look," the show's host directed. "He has a scar on his right lip, an eight-inch scar on his back, near his shoulder blade, and he walks with a slight limp."

Nearly 500 calls poured in. Many were tips from Staten Islanders. Convinced that Lord and Roberts were the same man, the FBI impounded the blue sedan that Lord used to deliver homeless people from the cold.

One woman who remembered Lord's good deeds helped him elude the FBI. She was the mother of a four-year-old son, and Roberts had helped her when she was homeless. She believed the story he told her, that the police were hounding him but had the wrong man. She agreed to hide him in her apartment.

The FBI was convinced that without money or a car, Roberts couldn't go far. Fourteen agents scoured Staten Island for the 44-year-old fugitive.

When they learned where Roberts was hiding, agents picked up the woman outside her son's school and brought her in for questioning. She denied that she knew where Roberts was. But FBI agents trusted their own information and crept into the apartment building. When the agents knocked, Roberts threw his weight against the door to block their entry, but soon relented.

Roberts was led out in handcuffs, his head hanging over his chest. On February 11, the double life of David Roberts and Bob Lord merged into one.

| Back | Forward | Home | Reload | Images | Open | Print | Find | Stop |

Location: http://www.fbi.gov/mostwant/rogge.htm

| What's New? | What's Cool? | Destinations | Net Search | People | Software |

FBI HOME | MORE INFO | PHOTOS | TOP TEN | NEXT FUG. | FAQs | FBI OFFICES

the FBI's ten most wanted fugitives

Photograph taken 1989

ARMED AND DANGEROUS

Bank Robbery; Interstate Transportation of Stolen Property; Fraud by Wire

Leslie Isben Rogge

aka: J. Carpenter, Rodney William Dickens, Leslie Gibseen, Leslie Isben Moore, Robert Charles Nelson, Fred Pratts, Wally Preston, Leslie Gibson Rogle, Donald Clark Rose, Donald King Williams, and others.

THE CRIME:

<u>Leslie Isben Rogge</u>, an escapee from custody, is being sought for a series of bank robberies in which a handgun was used.

No Place
Left to Hide

The arrest of David James Roberts electrified viewers and touched off a new era of televised dragnets. But FBI Top Tenners had not been strangers to TV.

Ushering in the electronic chase was a fictional show, *The F.B.I.*, which ran for nine years starting in 1965. FBI director J. Edgar Hoover used the series, which was based on actual FBI cases, to promote the bureau. He handpicked actor Efrem Zimbalist, Jr., to play the leading role of Inspector Erskine. At the end of each episode, Zimbalist read through the Most Wanted list in an appeal for information from viewers.

In 1987 the line between TV and reality grew even thinner with the premiere of NBC's *Unsolved Mysteries*. This show was the first in the United States to enlist the public's help in catching the fugitives it profiled. It even employed actor Robert Stack, TV's original Eliot Ness, as narrator.

The FBI continues to work with producers to flesh

Global crime-fighting village: When the FBI posted pictures of Leslie Rogge on its World Wide Web site, an Internet browser in Guatemala recognized the fugitive and alerted police. Rogge had spent six years on the Top Ten list after escaping from federal authorities in Idaho.

51

out segments on Most Wanted and other fugitives. Viewers have led police to two Top Tenners profiled on the show.

Unsolved Mysteries devotes about a third of its shows to fugitives, but most episodes center on missing persons, lost loves, and unexplained deaths.

In 1988 the spotlight burned brighter on fugitives with the advent of *America's Most Wanted*, a reality-based show that netted both criminals and ratings. But getting the show on the air was no easy feat.

The show's producers had envisioned a program that would reconstruct crimes using actors along with real-life witnesses and detectives. Urgent drumbeat soundtracks would pipe in the tension. The fugitive's photograph would flash onto the screen. Then viewers could call a toll-free number with tips.

It was an ambitious plan, and the FBI was cautious. In fact, the bureau's public affairs department at first declined to cooperate with the producers of *America's Most Wanted*. The FBI feared that the show would jeopardize its cases by getting facts wrong or sensationalizing crimes.

Without FBI cooperation, the show's producers hit a wall. So they took the next step, appealing to Oliver B. "Buck" Revell, the FBI's chief of operations. Revell was willing to give the show a chance after producers agreed to give the FBI some control.

"They understood our problems with the show and decided to make it useful to law enforcement, and not sensational," Revell recalled.

Instead of hiring an actor to narrate the show, *America's Most Wanted* recruited victims' rights advocate John Walsh. He knew firsthand the pain of losing a loved one to a murderer. His six-year-old son, Adam, was abducted from a Hollywood, Florida, store in 1981. Two weeks later, the boy's mutilated body was found by a stream 150 miles away.

The FBI provided photographs and information on

David James Roberts for the pilot program. The TV crew reconstructed Roberts's arson murder and his gunpoint escape from custody. Agents helped field phone calls from viewers. To everyone's surprise, it took only four days to reel in the fugitive.

The Roberts capture convinced federal law enforcement and producers at *America's Most Wanted* that TV could help bring fugitives to justice. But it was the case of John Emil List that put the show on the map in 1989.

List was a quiet, churchgoing accountant who in November 1971 snapped. He fatally shot his wife, mother, and three children, wiped up the blood, and laid the bodies neatly, side by side, on top of sleeping bags in the living room of the family's crumbling suburban mansion in New Jersey. He switched the radio on to classical music and departed, boarding a plane at

Actor Efrem Zimbalist, Jr. (third from left), as Inspector Erskine in the TV series The F.B.I., *which ran from 1965 to 1974. After each episode, Zimbalist read through the Most Wanted list, marking the first regular use of broadcast media to publicize the cases of Top Tenners.*

John Emil List is led into court in Richmond, Virginia, in August 1989. Eighteen years earlier, List had murdered his mother, wife, and children and slipped into obscurity. After his crime was featured on America's Most Wanted, *viewers recognized him as a quiet accountant who called himself Robert Clark and lived in Midlothian, Virginia.*

Kennedy Airport and slipping into obscurity for nearly 18 years.

As heinous as his crime was, List never made the Most Wanted lineup. Still, the FBI worked very closely with the show's creators to furnish them with information.

The night List was profiled, *America's Most Wanted* unveiled a plaster bust of the fugitive as the artist believed he might look 18 years after his disappearance. The bust bore a striking resemblance to the 63-year-old accountant who was living with a new wife in Midlothian, Virginia, under the assumed name of Robert P. Clark.

Hundreds of calls flooded the switchboard, including one that supplied the FBI with List's alias and address. Eleven days later, FBI agents confronted Clark at the accounting firm where he worked. He denied he was John List, but his fingerprints gave him away. He was later found guilty of the murders of his family and is serving five consecutive life sentences in prison.

It didn't take long for the FBI to embrace *America's Most Wanted* with enthusiasm. In 1989 FBI director William Sessions even made a rare TV appearance on the show, hailing the program as a public service.

One thing was for sure: a TV posse of millions watching from their living rooms made it harder for fugitives to hide behind new hairstyles, mustaches, and covered-up tattoos.

"With 40 million pairs of eyes helping you find a fugitive, you're a lot better off," said FBI spokesman Rex Tomb.

TV soon became the FBI's preferred mode of publicity. Though a newspaper reporter helped kindle the Most Wanted program in 1949, TV was getting the scoops in the 1990s.

In 1991 the FBI cut a deal with the producers of *Unsolved Mysteries* and *America's Most Wanted* to give them exclusives on new additions to the Most Wanted list.

When a newspaper reporter asked for the name of the latest fugitive, an FBI spokeswoman told the reporter to catch it on TV.

"The day you guys can deliver up 60 million households, we'll work exclusively with you," the spokeswoman said. "It's the most efficient way."

The FBI pointed out that newspapers can't match the element of surprise provided by TV. A new fugitive could be shown in an instant to a huge TV audience, setting the stage for a swift capture.

During its initial eight-year run, *America's Most Wanted* helped the FBI nab 431 fugitives, including 11 Top Tenners. And it revived interest in the FBI's Most Wanted program, which had been waning. In fact, between 1970 and 1988—*America's Most Wanted*'s first season on the air—citizen help figured in only 12 percent of the captures, down from 36 percent during the first 20 years of the FBI's Most Wanted list.

The appeal of living-room crime fighting was no doubt heightened by the updates aired whenever a fugitive profiled on *America's Most Wanted* was captured. Viewers could see concrete results; they could know when cases had been closed, something that is often difficult to find out from print media such as newspapers and magazines.

The popularity of *America's Most Wanted* has spurred imitators on local network news affiliates—along with concerns that the dramatizations could violate the rights of the accused. Critics say the shows present a one-sided account of the crime, pegging the blame on someone who could be completely innocent.

Marshall Blonsky, a professor at New York's New School for Social Research, likened the reenactments to game shows that enlist mobs to play.

"It distracts the population by giving people enormous sadistic pleasure," Blonsky maintained. "There's something really unnecessarily mean about these programs. They treat fugitives like cockroaches with phrases like 'You can run but you can't hide.'"

Others worry that jurors deciding the fate of a defendant could be swayed by televised depictions of the gruesome crimes.

Or, as in the case of Robin John Delgado, the wrong person could be arrested. Delgado, a Los Angeles bartender, was hauled in after being mistaken for a fugitive profiled on *America's Most Wanted*. He sued the TV show, the Los Angeles Police Department, and the FBI, alleging that he was libeled and falsely imprisoned.

Critics claim that the cozy relationship between the producers and the FBI crosses an ethical line. Journalists should be watchdogs of law enforcement, not partners, they say.

America's Most Wanted spokeswoman Kathy Swanda has argued that the program is a "victim's advocacy show," not journalism in the traditional sense.

WANTED BY THE FBI

ARMED AND DANGEROUS

WHITE MALE
48 YEARS OLD
5'10"
190 LBS.
GRAY HAIR
BROWN EYES
SEVERAL TATTOOS

KENNETH O'DONNELL
aka KENNETH MARINO

CALL YOUR LOCAL FBI OFFICE

For people like retired FBI assistant director Revell, the bottom line is that the shows help rid the streets of dangerous criminals. "I think there are dozens of people alive today that wouldn't be alive [if not for] that program," he said.

Revell said the shows offer an alternative to vigilantism by giving viewers the chance to call the FBI and let the bureau handle arrests. Other supporters say a jury would never be tainted because there will always be people who haven't seen the depictions.

David James Roberts, who is now doing life in the Indiana State Prison, entered the debate in 1989 during his appearance on the one-year anniversary show of *America's Most Wanted*.

Roberts, who was interviewed from prison, has maintained his innocence in the murders and the rape, saying he was the victim of a racist Indiana justice system. He asked Walsh how he could sleep at night knowing that he might have helped put innocent people behind bars.

"I've thought of it continually, and I believe in the

In June 1994 moviegoers in 58 New York City theaters saw these mug shots of Kenneth "Kenny the Rat" O'Donnell before the feature-film presentations. Although the publicity led to the convicted mobster's arrest, theater owners have balked at letting the FBI profile other fugitives on the big screen.

criminal justice system," Walsh said.

In May 1996 Fox announced that it would drop *America's Most Wanted* to make room for new programming. The cancellation stirred such an outcry that Fox producers changed their minds.

Four months later, Fox Entertainment president Peter Roth issued a news release declaring that he would bring back the series. "There has been an enormous outpouring from law enforcement agencies, government officials—including governors of 37 states—and viewers asking us to keep *America's Most Wanted* on the air," he said.

"Never before has a television program made such a clear and significant impact on people's lives. Quite simply, people have told us that this program made them feel safer."

TV boosted the public's interest in the Most Wanted list, but law enforcement continues to look down new avenues to find fugitives. The FBI is using cutting-edge technology to spotlight criminals at large. Its two newest projects ask people from all over the world to be on the lookout for dangerous criminals.

The FBI plans to profile fugitives in three-minute spots on Voice of America, a radio network with an international audience of 100 million listeners.

"The world's getting smaller, and you have more people that go overseas," said FBI spokesman Tomb.

Instead of relying on photographs, the FBI will describe Top Tenners who agents believe have fled U.S. borders. "We'll have to paint a picture for the radio audience by using very specific details," Tomb said.

Another publicity project—sending mug shots into cyberspace—has already yielded results. The FBI caught a fugitive on the World Wide Web (a network of computer links that enables people to access databases from a personal computer) for the first time in May 1996. Leslie Rogge had been convicted of armed robbery. After escaping from federal custody in Idaho, he spent six years on the FBI's Most Wanted list. A person browsing the Internet in Guatemala recognized Rogge's picture and notified police there. A massive manhunt ensued, and Rogge, feeling the heat, turned himself in.

The FBI regularly searches for as many as 6,000 fugitives from justice. The bureau plans to upload more of their faces onto the Internet. "We don't want it to look like a high school yearbook, we want to keep the numbers down," said Tomb, explaining that the FBI plans to use the World Wide Web judiciously.

The FBI's publicity campaigns haven't been limited to small screens. In June 1994 the bureau ran out of leads in the hunt for Kenneth O'Donnell, a convicted mobster who had escaped from the Passaic County jail in New Jersey. Agents suspected that O'Donnell, known as "Kenny the Rat," was hiding out in New York City. That summer, moviegoers in 58 New York theaters witnessed an eye-opening preview. In addition to the coming attractions and warnings not to smoke, they saw mug shots of the Rat.

O'Donnell was seized, but the FBI hasn't had much luck convincing theater owners to showcase more fugitives. The owners say that the Most Wanted notices put a damper on the moviegoing experience.

Newspapers have stood the test of time as crime stoppers, and the FBI hasn't written them off. Reporters still write stories when fugitives are added to the list and again when they're caught.

But when news isn't breaking in a long, drawn-out search for a fugitive, the FBI has paid big bucks for a spot in print. In several cases, the bureau bought ad space in national newspapers to get a fugitive's face before the public.

That strategy bore fruit in March 1996, after the trail went cold on a white-collar fugitive who had spent more than $2 million in bad checks. The FBI paid $3,000 to run an ad for two days in the *USA*

Today weekend edition. A reader called in a tip that led to the arrest of Scott Stefan Atkins in Beverly Hills, California.

Be it newspapers, radio, television, or cyberspace, the media have made the world a much tougher place in which to hide. The list of the FBI's Ten Most Wanted Fugitives started as a public relations ploy and grew into an important investigative tool that has helped the FBI haul in hundreds of fugitives.

In a country fascinated with crime and violence, the FBI's Ten Most Wanted Fugitives has become an American icon. On any given day or night, hundreds of fugitives will be running from the law and millions of eyes will be watching.

Appendix

Appendix

An FBI True-or-False Quiz

1 The FBI is a kind of national police force.

❏ TRUE
❏ FALSE

2 The FBI investigates all violations of federal and constitutional law.

❏ TRUE
❏ FALSE

3 If a crime is a violation of both local and federal laws, the FBI takes over the investigation because federal law takes precedence.

❏ TRUE
❏ FALSE

4 Even though it has no authority over local law enforcement agencies, the FBI can be called in to investigate a serious crime, such as murder, when local police can't solve the case.

❏ TRUE
❏ FALSE

5 The FBI assists local law enforcement agencies by sharing information and resources.

❏ TRUE
❏ FALSE

6 FBI agents have authority to make arrests.

❑ TRUE
❑ FALSE

7 After the FBI has completed an investigation, it decides whether the evidence warrants further action or prosecution.

❑ TRUE
❑ FALSE

8 The FBI issues security clearances to government officials who work in highly sensitive positions.

❑ TRUE
❑ FALSE

9 The FBI investigates possible civil rights violations.

❑ TRUE
❑ FALSE

10 If a child is missing under circumstances that point to a possible kidnapping, the FBI may begin an investigation even though there is no evidence of interstate transportation.

❑ TRUE
❑ FALSE

Turn the page to check your answers.

Answers to
An FBI True-or-False Quiz

1. The FBI is a kind of national police force.

❏ TRUE
☑ FALSE

The FBI is not a police force. It is a fact-finding organization that investigates violations of federal law.

2. The FBI investigates all violations of federal and constitutional law.

❏ TRUE
☑ FALSE

The FBI may investigate only if a possible violation falls within the bureau's jurisdiction (which is defined by laws passed by Congress) or if instructed to do so by the U.S. president or the U.S. attorney general.

3. If a crime is a violation of both local and federal laws, the FBI takes over the investigation because federal law takes precedence.

❏ TRUE
☑ FALSE

State and local police agencies aren't subordinate to the FBI, and the bureau has no authority to take control of their investigations. In cases in which both local and federal laws have been violated, the FBI and local police work together.

4. Even though it has no authority over local law enforcement agencies, the FBI can be called in to investigate a serious crime, such as murder, when local police can't solve the case.

❏ TRUE
☑ FALSE

Unless a crime falls within the FBI's well-defined jurisdiction, the bureau has no power to investigate, even if local authorities request that it do so.

5. **The FBI assists local law enforcement agencies by sharing information and resources.**

    ☑ TRUE
    ❏ FALSE

The FBI maintains one of the most sophisticated crime-detection labs in the world, and local agencies frequently rely on it to examine and analyze evidence. In addition, the FBI shares information through the Criminal Justice Information Services Division and the National Center for the Analysis of Violent Crime. And the bureau's Behavioral Science Unit, which has developed profiles of serial killers, maintains a national data base of unsolved murders that local agencies can access.

6. **FBI agents have authority to make arrests.**

    ☑ TRUE
    ❏ FALSE

Agents may make arrests by warrant. They may also make arrests without a warrant if a federal offense has been committed in their presence or if they believe the person to be arrested has committed or is attempting to commit a felony violation of U.S. laws.

7. **After the FBI has completed an investigation, it decides whether the evidence warrants further action or prosecution.**

    ❏ TRUE
    ☑ FALSE

Upon completion of an investigation, the FBI presents the facts of the case to the appropriate U.S. attorney or Department of Justice official, who determines how to proceed.

8. The FBI issues security clearances to government officials who work in highly sensitive positions.

❑ TRUE
☑ FALSE

The FBI issues security clearances only to its own employees. At the request of other government agencies, the bureau does conduct background checks of applicants for jobs requiring security clearance, but the decision on whether or not to grant clearance rests with the agency that is filling the job.

9. The FBI investigates possible civil rights violations.

☑ TRUE
❑ FALSE

The FBI conducts civil rights investigations, turning its results over to the Department of Justice for follow-up.

10. If a child is missing under circumstances that point to a possible kidnapping, the FBI may begin an investigation even though there is no evidence of interstate transportation.

☑ TRUE
❑ FALSE

The law stipulates that unless the victim is located or released within 24 hours, it may be presumed that he or she has been transported across state lines.

Breslin, Jack. *America's Most Wanted*. New York: Harper Paperbacks, 1990.

Charns, Alexander. *Cloak and Gavel*. Chicago: University of Illinois Press, 1992.

Garrow, David J. *The FBI and Martin Luther King, Jr.* New York: W. W. Norton & Co., 1981.

Gentry, Curt. *J. Edgar Hoover: The Man and the Secrets*. New York: Norton, 1991.

Israel, Fred L. *The FBI*. New York: Chelsea House, 1986.

Lynum, Curtis O. *The FBI and I: One Family's Life in the FBI During the Hoover Years*. Bryn Mawr, Pa.: Dorrance & Co., 1988.

Newton, Michael, and Judy Ann Newton. *The FBI Most Wanted*. New York: Dell Publishing, 1989.

O'Reilly, Kenneth. Racial Matters: *The FBI's Secret File on Black America, 1960–1972.* New York: The Free Press, 1989.

Overstreet, Harry, and Bonaro Overstreet. *The FBI in Our Open Society*. New York: W. W. Norton & Co., 1969.

Powers, Richard Gid. *G-Men: Hoover's FBI in American Popular Culture*. Carbondale: Southern Illinois University Press, 1983.

Summers, Anthony. *Official and Confidential*. New York: G. P. Putnam's Sons, 1993.

Theoharis, Athan, and John Stuart Cox. *The Boss*. Philadelphia: Temple University Press, 1988.

Turner, William. *Hoover's FBI: The Men and the Myth*. Los Angeles: Sherbourne Press, 1970.

Ungar, Sanford. *FBI*. Boston: Atlantic Monthly Press, 1975.

Welch, Neil, and David Marston. *Inside Hoover's FBI*. New York: Doubleday, 1984.

Index

Index

Picture Credits

Every effort has been made to contact the copyright owners of photographs and illustrations used in this book. In the event that the holder of a copyright has not heard from us, he or she should contact Chelsea House Publishers.

page

2: FBI's Internet Home Page	28: Courtesy The FBI	47: Courtesy *America's Most Wanted*
12-13: UPI/Bettmann	30: Courtesy The FBI	
15: Courtesy The FBI	34: Courtesy The FBI	48: Courtesy *America's Most Wanted*
16: Courtesy The FBI	37: AP/Wide World Photos	
19: UPI/Bettmann	39: UPI/Corbis-Bettmann	50: FBI's Internet Home Page
20: UPI/Corbis-Bettmann	41: AP/Wide World Photos	53: Corbis-Bettmann
22: UPI/Corbis-Bettmann	43: AP/Wide World Photos	54: AP/Wide World Photos
25: AP/Wide World Photos	44: Courtesy *America's Most Wanted*	57: Courtesy The FBI
26: UPI/Bettmann		cover photo: UPI/Bettmann

LAURA D'ANGELO is a freelance writer and editor living in New York City.

AUSTIN SARAT is William Nelson Cromwell Professor of Jurisprudence & Political Science at Amherst College, where he also chairs the Department of Law, Jurisprudence and Social Thought. Professor Sarat is the author or editor of 22 books and numerous scholarly articles. Among his books are *Law's Violence*, *Sitting in Judgment: Sentencing the White Collar Criminal*, and *Justice and Injustice in Law and Legal Theory*. He has received many academic awards and held several prestigious fellowships. In addition, he is a nationally recognized teacher and educator whose teaching has been featured in the *New York Times*, on the *Today* show, and on National Public Radio's *Fresh Air*.